DECLUTTERING MADE EASY

A Simple Step-by-Step Guide

Jane Higgins

GW00480797

ARTHUR H. STOCKWELL LTD
Torrs Park, Ilfracombe, Devon, EX34 8BA
Established 1898
www.ahstockwell.co.uk

© *Jane Higgins, 2018*
First published in Great Britain, 2018

The moral rights of the author have been asserted.

All rights reserved.
No part of this publication may be reproduced
or transmitted in any form or by any means,
electronic or mechanical, including photocopy,
recording, or any information storage and
retrieval system, without permission
in writing from the copyright holder.

British Library Cataloguing-in-Publication Data.
A catalogue record for this book is available
from the British Library.

ISBN 978-0-7223-4888-8
Printed in Great Britain by
Arthur H. Stockwell Ltd
Torrs Park   Ilfracombe
Devon EX34 8BA

CONTENTS

DEDICATION

I would like to dedicate this, my first book, to several very important people in my life.

First and foremost, to my wonderful family: my husband, Rob, and our children, Nicole and Matthew. For their constant love, care, support and encouragement, especially during the very difficult times of huge emotional upheaval; for keeping me grounded and sane, by taking me out to the moors and countryside, which helped me to see the bigger picture, giving me a more positive perspective when everything looked bleak.

To my brother, David Greeves, for giving me the impetus I needed to start sorting things out, instead of just moving them from place to place! Also, for reallocating and selling almost all of the furniture; for his love, support, patience and understanding during what was a horrendous time for us both after our mum's death.

To our late mum's best friend, Carole Bedford, who helped us to sort, clear and empty our mum's house after her death. She stayed with us, and kept us calm from beginning to end; showed us how to make each task a little easier by breaking it down into smaller chunks; always worked very hard without complaint; and reduced the immense, extremely intense emotional stress by using sensible advice and good memories.

To our late mum's neighbour, Hilary Greene, for helping to care for our mum and for always being there when she was needed by her. As well as for her help, support, reassurance and advice during our struggle to clear Mum's house, and for her wonderful friendship since.

To all of our late mum's friends for all their years of friendship to her, and to us after her death. Also, for their support, advice and encouragement, which was much appreciated.

To our friends and neighbours, Mr and Mrs Mayman, for their help, support and understanding during this very lengthy process; and not forgetting their huge contribution towards the redistribution and relocation of 1,000-plus books!

To Mr and Mrs Rowles for all their lifts, advice and encouragement.

Also, to all the wonderful people I have met during this prolonged and painful process, all of whom have been encouraging, supportive and helpful. From Saltash town councillors, Saltash Heritage and St Luke's Charity Shop in Saltash, to shopkeepers on the Barbican, Plymouth, to various army addresses and archives, and to Bedford Council, Bedford Records Office and its archivist, plus the fabulous St Agnes playgroup 'girls'.

Thank you so much to all of you: I couldn't have done it without you.

Last, but not least, to our late mum, Hazel Greeves, for her love and care over the years for us, her children, and for her enduring loyalty to many different local organisations in Saltash, which gave her so much pleasure throughout her life. Also for inadvertently turning me into a declutterer, by keeping everything!

PROLOGUE

This is my first ever book, which I wrote as a result of my personal experience, after having completed decluttering and emptying my late mum's home. I did this with the invaluable help of my brother, David Greeves; our Mum's best friend, Carole Bedford; plus Mum's neighbour, Hilary Greene.

Our mum's home was packed to the rafters, and beyond, with everything kept from early married days, our babyhood, childhood and more recently! As a result, it was a totally overwhelming task for us to sort through – in time required, on-site and at our own homes, sorting what we had brought back with us, as well as being both physically and emotionally draining.

We all found it extremely stressful, which was worsened by not being able to find any evidence of her funeral having been arranged or paid for. It took us nine months to clear the house!

The house looked so different and spacious once it was completed. It was such a shame that Mum hadn't allowed us to help her to declutter when she was alive and well, as it would have had a hugely beneficial impact on her life, especially as it would have made her home environment much safer than it had been. I also feel that she would probably have liked the new, decluttered look, but possibly felt too ashamed to ask for help and found the enormous task far too difficult and painful to undertake or contemplate.

Through this very difficult process, I felt that I had learnt an incredible amount about our mum and myself. I also learnt about the necessity and importance of decluttering, as well as various methods of doing so.

I felt that this knowledge was much too important to keep to myself, and by sharing it through the medium of a handy-sized paperback book, I might be able to encourage others to welcome the process of decluttering into their lives.

Although this book is more probably aimed at those of the fifty-plus age group, it would be helpful to the younger generation too. For example, in supporting their parents through the often very painful process of downsizing to a smaller home; for a general moving-home aid; and to encourage the younger generation to reuse, upcycle and recycle unwanted belongings, especially when leaving their childhood home or setting up their own home; also in illustrating the importance of considering the future, even though it might not seem very relevant at the moment.

I wrote this book prior to doing any research about whether there were any similar books available on the market, as I didn't want my writing style to be influenced in any way, and felt that it was best to write from the heart.

I hope that you all enjoy both reading this book and using the book to its full potential. Happy decluttering!

INTRODUCTION

Is the place that you live somewhere that you are proud of and pleased with, so that you could happily receive an unannounced visitor at any time? Or is it somewhere that fills you with dread, as you feel too ashamed to invite anyone at all?

If the latter is the case, then this book could be very useful to you, as a simple step-by-step guide for learning how to declutter.

Learning to declutter, and becoming an ardent activist for the need to declutter, has literally changed my life. I would like to pass these lessons on to you, and to inspire you to do the same.

So, instead of looking at your mess and feeling overwhelmed, disheartened and depressed, you will see it as a challenge and something to be overcome. It will be difficult to do, and actually starting to do it is the worst part, but decluttering will result in a very positive outcome for you, as you will feel much happier and more content to spend time in your own home. This will also be something which your family and friends will greatly appreciate too, as they will feel more welcome and more able to relax in your home as well.

You will also find that you feel much happier in yourself,

as you will be able to relax more and enjoy life, rather than constantly worrying about, and being held back by, your own clutter. You need to declutter to feel free! So, are you ready? Let's get going and set to work.

CHAPTER ONE

What Is Clutter?

Clutter is defined as 'things lying around untidily'. However, I would also define it as anything which you no longer need in your everyday life.

How Does the Clutter Make You Feel?

How do you really feel when you see your clutter? You need to be honest with yourself to answer this question. Do you feel ashamed, upset and distressed? Does it make you feel angry and cross with yourself for allowing it to build up like this? And do you now feel guilty about it? Would you feel happy allowing anyone into your home unannounced, or do you find that you have to rush around closing doors, drawers and cupboards to contain and conceal the chaos? Or are you quite happy for everyone to see the mess that you live in, and you don't get upset by it or by what others may say about it?

If the latter is the case, then perhaps you are in denial about your clutter, or just feel that it is far too much for anyone to deal with. Don't despair – hope is here in this book, and help may be willingly given by friends and family if only you can ask for it.

Why Do You Have Clutter in Your Home?

This might be worth thinking about, especially as the answers might provide the key to releasing you from future hoarding and further clutter.

Did you have an upsetting childhood? Did you feel isolated, insecure and unloved? Were you bullied, belittled and mocked? Were you adopted and although loved by your new family, felt as if you were unworthy of their love? Was something that you treasured taken from you against your will and destroyed, as you were just a child at the time, without a voice?

Have you lost a loved one and felt unable to cope? Does keeping their belongings and their written paperwork help you to feel closer to them, more secure and safe?

What about your children's belongings, including much loved toys, books and clothes, even though they are now much older, or even with their own families, and moved out of your family home many years ago? Does having their possessions around you make them and the many happy memories feel closer?

Perhaps asking yourself some of these questions will help you to discover an underlying and long-hidden problem which you either hadn't realised you had, or had denied having for very many years. If you feel that these are problems which you are unable to deal with by yourself, by talking openly to your family and friends, perhaps it would be a good idea to speak to your doctor, who could refer you for counselling.

CHAPTER TWO

Why Do You Need to Declutter?

1.   To make more space in your home.

2.   To make it easier for you to clean and to keep clean.

3.   To make it a safer and healthier environment for you, especially as you are getting older, less mobile and more vulnerable.

4.   To make your home a more pleasant place to be, for yourself, your family and friends, for whenever anyone visits.

5.   So that the atmosphere in your home is one of peace – a place to relax, not a place in which both friends and relatives feel worried, concerned and unsettled due to your clutter overtaking the house and your life.

6.   To make it easier for your family if and when something happens to you. (Remember, they will be devastated at this time, and having the extra stress

and strain caused by having to sort through clutter will bring enormous emotional turmoil, which can feel completely overwhelming.)

7. To feel free, to uplift your mood, to feel as if you are in control of your life and your home.

8. To finally enjoy being in your own home and spending time in it, rather than running away from it by almost always being out!

9. To feel that your home belongs to you, and not your clutter!

Simple Rules for Decluttering

1. In order to declutter, you need to want to do it and act on it, instead of only thinking about doing it.

2. Set aside a day and time to start, as if you have an appointment, without any distractions.

3. Be properly prepared to declutter. Items you may need:
    - Pens and marker pens.
    - Plenty of scrap paper and newspaper.
    - Sticky tape, scissors and a staple-removing tool.
    - Rubbish bin.
    - Recycling bags.
    - Black rubbish bags.
    - An exercise book, notebook or large writing pad.
    - A good pair of gloves, to protect your hands.

The exercise book, notebook or large writing pad is for you to use as you wish. It could be for the room you are working on, where you are working and whichever part you are currently sorting out. You can jot down ideas about where to send your clutter; it could be used as a declutter diary, monitoring the days and times spent sorting out a particular room, so that you can add it up at the end; it could also act as a reminder of questions to ask yourself about your clutter. Perhaps you could also have a visual-icon diagram page of how you are feeling as you declutter a room: you may be amazed at how quickly your mood improves! It may be useful to have a list of possible outlets for your clutter in the back of the book, too.

4. You may also need a good chair to sit on and a table of a reasonable and comfortable height to work at, as well as some space to move around with access to your exit door, so you can stop for a tea or toilet break.

5. Take photos of each room and the contents before you start decluttering, as well as during the process and when you have completed each room. This will help to inspire you to continue, as you will be able to see the progress that you have made.

Golden Rules for Decluttering

1. Only do ONE room at a time, ONE job at a time, and ONE area of a room at a time.

2. Go at your own pace – whatever is comfortable and best for you in mind, body and spirit.

3. Take regular breaks, and take longer breaks if it all gets a bit overwhelming, but ALWAYS return to the same job until that job is finished.

4. When taking regular breaks, do whatever suits you best: perhaps ten minutes every hour, or half an hour every two hours. You will need these breaks as it can be very emotionally taxing and extremely tiring.

5. If you are taking a break, especially a long one, always tidy up in an organised way before leaving it. Therefore it will be much easier when you return to the sorting.

6. You can have someone to help you, such as a friend or relative. Do not feel too proud, ashamed or embarrassed to ask for help when you need it. Sometimes it is easier with a companion, as you can have a chat, a laugh, bounce ideas off each other and put problems into perspective, sometimes finding solutions. You may find this process quite stressful and upsetting, as it is very hard to let go of much loved possessions, so you may become angry, frustrated and irritable. Try not to get upset with your innocent assistant: remember, you did ask them for help, and they don't have to be there!

7. Perhaps start with the smallest room first, as this can look the worst. Once this is cleared it should give you a big boost, encouraging you to continue with this dreaded and sometimes mammoth task.

8. Always ensure that all plugs and sockets, including aerial and phone sockets, are kept clear of any inflammable materials in all of your rooms, even before you have begun any sorting.

CHAPTER THREE

Where Do You Start?

Before you even start sorting the smallest room first, as suggested earlier, you may feel at a loss about where and how to begin.

Depending on your personal circumstances and situation, the smallest room first may not be an option. Instead you may have to deal with the items which take up the most space first. In our case, these were the books in the lounge, which amounted to over 1,000! We then progressed on to sorting out which items of furniture were to be advertised for sale, before we could do any room-by-room sorting and clearance, as we had originally intended.

Is the first room which you decide to sort so bad that a mattress falls out when you open the door? Or can you only partially open a door, so that you shut it rapidly whilst trying to decide whether to laugh, cry or tear your hair out with frustration?

PLEASE DON'T DESPAIR! These are all completely natural reactions to what can be a totally overwhelming task, and **HELP IS HERE**. Take it one step at a time.

Helpful Tips Before You Begin

1. It is essential that you break the clearing and sorting jobs down into easy stages, as otherwise you can become quickly disheartened, lose interest and give up.

2. You may have the added stress, pressure and worry of needing to clear the house urgently. For example, if the last parent needs to move into a nursing home, or if the property is rented, so it needs to be either sold or relet quickly.

3. If you have reliable family members or friends who can help you, then the job will be completed much more quickly. However, having extra people can cause more friction and stress, so be very careful about whom you choose to ask.

4. Always remember to apologise quickly for any upsets caused as you are all distressed, grieving and frustrated. Many of us have very short tempers and say hurtful things, in the heat of the moment, which we really don't mean; and this is usually to those people we love the most. Remember that life is far too short, and we can all do with a warm and heartfelt hug.

5. It is very useful to have a 'Communications Book', especially if people work on different days on-site. It is essential to keep this up to date. You could record which room you are working on and whether you have found anything of interest, and that this needs to be checked through by everyone. You could also

list what you have done each day, and suggest the next task. If you all work together as a team, whether on-site at the same time or not, the job will be finished much more quickly.

For the items which need checking by everyone, perhaps you could arrange a mutually convenient evening when this can be done, perhaps accompanied by a unifying buffet meal or takeaway in a more relaxed atmosphere. However, if this is impossible, you could use the Communications Book as a messaging service recording what each person thinks, who has seen or read it, and their thoughts about what to do with particular items. You could make doubly sure that this is dealt with by labelling the appropriate crate or box with contents to be read or seen by everyone. Obviously, you can phone, text and email each other too.

Starting to Sort an Appallingly Dreadful Room

This would include all the examples presented above!

1. If there is a mattress, inspect it for any damage, wear, stains and marks, as well as for any fire-regulation and 'CE' labels. If it is not fit for use, it needs to be moved and stored safely until it can be disposed of properly. This would either be by yourselves at the local council tip or by the local council's bulky waste collection service for large and bulky items.

2. The next step is to start by clearing the floor. You will need all your equipment ready, as described in Chapter Two, even if you need to start sorting a

room by being in the hallway or on the landing to begin with!

Put all paperwork together in a crate or several of these — preferably without reading it, as this will distract you from your task and will mean that it will take much longer! Do the same for everything else which is found on the floor too. If items on the floor are in different categories, such as bric-a-brac or small electrical items, then these need to be placed in separate crates for these items only. Label each crate clearly, showing the category and whether the items have been sorted or not.

3.   Using this method, clear enough floor space to allow you to work in the room itself. You will begin to feel as if you are getting somewhere, even though you haven't begun sorting through the contents yet! To give yourself a further boost, you could vac the area of cleared floor, so that it is ready for you to begin the sorting process in earnest.

4.   You should now be ready to face the challenge, as you will have organised yourself using the guidelines set out in Chapter Two. Perhaps have a motivational cup of tea first though, to see you through the next two hours of hard work; but start with the 'Needs Sorting' crates first. It may be best to leave the paperwork crates until last, as these will take the longest.

5.   If you are working by yourself, a radio is good company, especially if it has uplifting and motivational music.

Sorting the Different Categories

Almost all of the different categories presented here are covered in more detail in Chapter Four, but below is a 'quick-sort' guide.

All Paperwork

Unfortunately, dealing with any kind of paperwork takes an extraordinarily long time, and can contribute towards enormous negative feelings of pressure, stress and anxiety, making you feel like you want to give up. To prevent this from happening, perhaps keep putting all the paperwork into the crate for sorting through later. (Later can mean a few hours or a few days.) I found that little and often is best for paperwork. You do not want to stop this very important clearing process before it has even begun, and before you begin to feel any sense of real achievement.

Each piece of paperwork needs to be read and checked through thoroughly. Depending on what it is, it may need to be kept safely to one side for more intensive reading and investigation later; it may need to be torn up and put into the kitchen (food) bin; it may need to be recycled (ensure staples are removed); or it may need to be shredded. You will need to have a special labelled crate for all kept paperwork; but for all the paperwork which is being disposed of, as soon as a pile builds up, deal with it there and then as appropriate.

Ornaments and Bric-a-Brac

Ornaments and bric-a-brac need to be checked for condition and quality. Any which are broken or cracked, (unless they are damaged but also collectable), can be disposed of by wrapping in newspaper and putting in the dustbin.

If you are unable to do any research about whether these pieces could be collectable or not, either using the Internet or books, the best idea would be to keep them together in a labelled crate and, when you have finished the room, arrange an appointment to visit an auctioneer.

Auctioneers will give you unbiased and knowledgeable advice. Don't worry about wasting their time if everything you have taken is of no value: at least you will know what to do with it, and you'll know you haven't thrown anything valuable away. If you take an itemised list with you, this will help in your quest to find them a good home, if possible.

Furniture

For modern upholstered furniture to be reused and sold, it must be in good condition and have 'CE' and fire-regulation labels on it. If you can find accompanying purchase paperwork, such as guarantees, if still applicable, then that is a bonus.

There are many charities which recycle and reuse many types of furniture. However, if it is unsuitable for them, and you are unable to sell it or use it yourself, the local council has a bulky waste collection service which you can book for a small fee.

White Goods

White goods include fridges, freezers and cookers, and the rules are similar to those for furniture, above. If they are unsuitable for second-hand shops, and you are unable to sell them, you will again need to arrange a collection by the local council.

Glassware

Once again, check condition and quality. If broken or

chipped, glassware needs to be wrapped in newspaper and preferably recycled in the correct container, or thrown in the dustbin, properly wrapped to avoid injuries. If glass items are in good condition, local charities will be grateful for them.

Books

Sorting through books can take a very long time too, not just due to the memories some of them may evoke, but due to the quantity of books, too.

Check each book for condition and whether there is any paperwork enclosed. Read the paperwork in case it is important. Once read, deal with as per paperwork, above.

If the books are in excellent condition, the local library may be interested in a donation. If the books are in very good or good condition, local charity shops may be more appropriate.

If the books are in very poor condition, perhaps with bent, missing and ripped pages or covers, plus discoloured pages and edging, then these need to be recycled in the appropriate bags. However, if the books are extremely old, they may need researching to assess whether they have any value and are collectable. You may want to keep these or sell them.

Small Electricals

Check electrical goods for condition and 'CE' marks. If they are in good condition, the charity shops may be grateful. If they are in poor condition, take them to the local council tip.

Stationery, Cards and Stamps

If stationery items are in good condition, they can be

kept and shared around between family members and friends who would use them. (I still have a handful of stamps and some notelets, three years later!)

Toiletries
If unopened and unused, unless they have expiry dates, toiletries can be divided up and used by others. (Although these were also divided three ways, as was the stationery, I have only just finished using them all!)

Clothing
Obviously sorting out clothing can be a very painful process, due to many memories of happier times, but you can all choose which items of clothing you would like to keep, as you sort through it. Once again, everything which is going to be given to local charities must be in good condition and clean.

Bedding
The same applies to bedding (see 'Clothing', above).

Old Spectacles and Their Cases
Spectacles can be recycled at your local optician's.

Old Medicines
Medicines all need to be properly and safely disposed of. Take all of them to your local chemist, even if you don't usually visit this chemist. (I took a very heavy, and filled to the brim, shopping trolley of old medicines to the nearest chemist to my home, and felt so guilty and embarrassed as I don't usually use that chemist. It was even worse as some of the medicines were so old that they should have been in a museum!)

How to Begin Sorting a Room until It Is Finished

Now that you can sit comfortably in the room, perhaps start with a set of drawers.

1. Sort through one drawer at a time, properly, until it is empty. I found that what worked best for me was emptying the drawer completely and then sorting through the contents. I put each item found into the appropriate bag or crate, depending on what it was. As I created more mess by doing this, once the chaos was cleared away I felt so much more satisfied. Obviously, you need to find what method suits you best; but apply one which keeps you motivated to continue.

2. Once the first drawer is completed, it is much easier to do the rest in the same manner. You just apply the same method to all the other areas of the room until it is finished. For example, sort one set of drawers at a time, then perhaps a wardrobe, followed by cupboards, and don't forget any under-the-bed drawers or hidden spaces! You need to be certain that the room is clear before you move on to the next room.

Questions to Ask Yourself When Sorting Your Clutter

1. When did I last wear/look at/use/read this?

2. If I keep it, am I likely to wear it/look at it/use it/read it?

3. For clothes and jewellery: Does this still suit me? Does it still fit me? Is it still appropriate for my age? Do I really want to keep it and, if so, when will I wear it? If the answer to question 1 is more than a year, then it is highly unlikely that you will need to keep these items. Remember, you need to be HONEST with yourself, no matter how hard that may be.

4. Why am I keeping these items?

5. Do I have an emotional or sentimental attachment to them?

If you do have an emotional or sentimental attachment to any items, then you need to put them to one side and keep them all together. Store them carefully in a labelled storage container and review them properly in a year's time. To ensure that you remember, mark this on your calendar and in your diary and ensure that it is done. If after a year you still find it too painful to let these items go, then keep them safely for another year, but try not to have too many items in this category.

REMEMBER, decluttering is for your own good; it is not meant to be torturous or guilt-inducing. You DO NOT need to get rid of everything which you don't use. You are decluttering for *you*: to give yourself more space, to make your home easier to clean and safer. Once completed, this will uplift your mood so much that you will be amazed, and wonder why you never did it before! The old saying 'a clean and tidy room equals a clean and tidy mind' is absolutely true, as you will soon discover. Keep going – it really is worth it!

After You Have Sorted One Room

1. Congratulate yourself! You have done it! You have conquered what seemed to be impossible! You have faced what was a huge challenge – faced it head on – and won. VERY WELL DONE!

2. You now deserve a reward! This can be whatever suits you: some relaxing baking with an edible reward to have with your cuppa; a walk outside in the countryside (woods, fields, moors, coast, neighbourhood parks/ gardens or gardens of stately homes), observing the beauty around you. Relax and look around you. Listen to the birdsong. Take notice of the different colours of plants, flowers and trees. Find somewhere quiet and tranquil outside to curl up and read a book. Do whatever it takes to distract you from your recent task and have some quality 'me time'.

3. Once you have had some time away to properly recharge your batteries, you will then probably realise just how much you have achieved. How do you feel now? Do you feel uplifted, proud, pleased, amazed and incredulous? Such an achievement should lead you to feel so proud and relieved; and once they have established a base inside you, then these feelings will boost your own motivation to continue.

4. If you would like to, you could use this newly cleared room to store your decluttered items from other rooms; but do not allow them to build up. Preferably, clear these items out after you have finished each room. This should encourage you to continue the process of decluttering.

CHAPTER FOUR

Questions to Ask Yourself about the Decluttered Items

1. Are they in perfect condition?

2. Would someone else benefit from using them?

3. Can they be valued?

4. Are they of historical value or interest?

5. What age groups will use them?

6. Are they of *local* historical value or interest?

7. Are they old family items and if so does any of my family want them? If family members don't want them, what do I do with them?

What to Do Next

1. Look in your local newspapers and magazines

for any outlets for your items. Also look in phone directories and online using your computer. Make a note of names, addresses and phone numbers and what sort of items each potential outlet is interested in.

2. Take photos of anything you wish to try to sell locally and visit these places with the photos on your camera. If dealers are interested, you can return with your items at a later date to sell them. When you revisit, intending to sell your items, go prepared with an organised, itemised list of your goods, so that you can record their comments and the prices they are prepared to pay you for each one. This will act as a quick reference point for you, so you will know exactly where to take each item for the best price, or whether they need to be taken to a charity shop.

3. *Medical or Nursing Equipment*: Contact local doctors' surgeries, hospitals and local charities to enquire whether they can use it.

4. *Educational-Type Books*: These could be given to local nurseries, playgroups, primary schools and academies/comprehensives.

5. *Jewellery, Including Costume Jewellery*: This can be valued at local jewellers' and antique shops. Some buy it and sell it as it is, after cleaning; others buy it to melt it down. Do what you feel is right for you, and ask them what they intend to do with it. Remember, you can take it to more than one person before you decide where to sell it.

You do not need to rush to sort jewellery or to dispose of it. You can keep all the jewellery safely together, and tackle this once everything else has been dealt with, as it can be the cause of mixed emotions and memories.

6. *China, Glassware and Bric-a-Brac*: Take your camera with photos to various second-hand and antique-type shops, as before. The markets are constantly changing, so sometimes there is a demand for these items.

7. *Charity Shops*: Decide which items need to go to charity shops. They will take all sorts of eclectic items, including clothing. They usually sell clothing, bric-a-brac, glassware, china, pictures and paintings, books, toys, jewellery, small electrical items and bedding. Some charities even have a collection service for larger items of furniture. They are always very grateful for your donations, but prefer them to be in good condition and 'CE' marks are required on all toys and electrical items.

If you are a taxpayer you can sign up to be a Gift Aid donor. This is a very quick process and only takes about five minutes to do. This will mean that for every pound your donations raise for the charity, the charity will be paid twenty-five pence tax-free by the government! All of your donations are marked with your individual Gift Aid label, and once a year the charity informs you of how much your donations have raised for the charity. This is all at no personal cost to you, and you can even be registered for Gift Aid at different shops!

8. **Auctioneers**: Make contact with auctioneers in person, by phone or via websites.

9. **Websites**: Search for useful websites using a computer. There may be useful local-area websites and free-for-collection websites, as well as eBay and more.

10. **Adverts**: These are more successful if they are accompanied by photos and good descriptions. They can be put in local newsagents, newspapers and magazines.

11. **Recycling**: All paper (including brown paper), cardboard, glass, plastic drinks cartons, tins and cans, plus tinfoil can be recycled.

12. **Non-Recyclables**: Anything which cannot be recycled, upcycled or reused in any way, by any of the aforementioned methods, means or businesses, can be taken to the local tip.

13. **Bulky Waste**: Arrange with your local council for removal of large pieces of furniture, fridges, freezers, etc. To find out details, you can visit or phone your town council or county council, or visit their website. You may be able to visit your local library and find out details from their one-stop shop on council-related matters too.

When You Have Decided What to Do with Your Discarded Items

1. Take them away from your home to the various designated places. You do not need to do this in one go! You can do this gradually, but steadily. Keep going until it has all left your home.

2. Once it has all gone, treat yourself and give yourself a huge pat on the back for a job well done.

3. Now you can complete the job, by giving that room a thorough clean!

How do you feel now that you have a wonderful light, airy and more spacious, clean and tidy room? Do you feel really good about yourself and about what you have achieved?

You should feel incredibly proud of yourself. That was a massive challenge, but you have managed to deal with it, and have done it at your own pace and for yourself. Allow that feeling to sink in and become part of you. Now that the task is over, how do you feel? Do you feel lighter? Has the weight that you were carrying on your head, neck and shoulders reduced as your stress levels have lowered? Do you feel better in yourself for letting go of your clutter?

CONGRATULATIONS! Rejoice in being the new you; welcome that feeling of new-found lightness and energy. You are turning over a new leaf in your life: YOU ARE A DECLUTTERER!

Welcome to my new world of happiness and positivity, kindness and joy in life.

CHAPTER FIVE

Sorting the Kitchen

Questions to ask yourself before you start:

1. How many of these cookery books do I actually use?

2. Which saucepans, baking equipment, crockery, utensils and cooking pots do I really use?

3. Which cleaning products do I actually use on a regular basis?

4. When did I last review the contents of my medicine cupboard?

Possible answers:

1. ***Cookery Books***: Keep the books which you use on a daily, weekly, occasional and special-events basis. Read through the rest and make notes on any recipes which you believe you will use in the future. Notes can be made in an exercise book devoted to

that purpose, or on your computer, tablet or iPad. Once your notes are completed, the unwanted cookery books can be recycled or taken to a charity shop of your choice.

2. **Cooking Equipment**: Make a note of any of these items that you have never used, and review them in three months' time. If you haven't used them by then, it is very unlikely that you ever will, so ideally these can be sold, taken to a charity shop, given to friends, a school or local college, or recycled.

3. **Cleaning Products**: You may be surprised at the variety and multitude of cleaning products you actually have. I know that I was! Once the cupboard was empty, I made a list of all the products, indicating what they were used for, how well they worked and if I would buy them again. The list is kept on the freezer for easy reference. The cupboard was refilled with similar products kept together in old ice-cream tubs. Therefore it has been much easier to find the products and use them up one at a time. Once they are used up, the cupboard will be half empty!

4. **Medicines**: It is best to sort medicines on at least a monthly basis, possibly even every two weeks. Old ice-cream and margarine tubs are ideal for keeping the medicine cupboard tidy and easy to manage.
Check all medicines for expiry dates and put a ring around them in pen, as well as writing the expiry dates on the front of the medicines to make them easier for you to read. Any expired medicines of

any kind, including used-up sprays or inhalers, must be disposed of properly and safely by taking them to a chemist. **DO NOT** put them in a bin as they can be dangerous.

A list of any 'soon to be needed' medicines can be made at the same time. If you have a tendency to forget when you took in a prescription to the chemist, make a note of the date and what it was for and put it on your fridge/freezer.

If you have any repeat-prescription slips, check through them for expiry dates and shred any which are out of date. Keep the rest together in a safe place, plus any exemption certificates too. Perhaps place them in a large labelled envelope. Ensure that your family know where they are kept too.

If you have any medical conditions such as allergies or take several medicines, it might be a good idea to summarise these on a postcard, with your details, attaching an up-to-date repeat-prescription list too. Therefore, if you go away on holiday, or are unfortunate enough to have to go to hospital, you will have all your essential details with you. However, make sure that you get it returned to you as quickly as possible. You can also record all these details on a separate piece of paper at home, kept with the medicine details.

Sorting the Attic and Garage

Questions to ask yourself before you start:

1.   When did I last look in here properly?

2. Do I know what is in here?

3. Have I missed what is stored in here?

4. Is it of any use and do I really need it?

5. How long has it been stored in here?

6. Can I be honest with myself when sorting through these items?

Once again, if the answer to the first question is over a year, you probably don't need any of it.

If the items stored belong to your children, especially if they are growing up, or are grown-up, then contact them to ask for their help sorting through them. If they don't come to help you, for whatever reason, box up their belongings with contents labels showing whom the items belong to, and store the boxes safely. Therefore, they will be ready for them to sort through whenever they do visit you. Before boxing and storing them, you could take photos of the items and email the photos to them. Ask them to give you instructions about what they would like you to do with them.

Do be strict with them and emphasise that you would like your space cleared, especially as it is far easier for them to do it now, with you, rather than after you have died, when their emotions will be in turmoil. Explain that you need to do this now in order to make it easier for them when that day occurs.

Ideally, you should just have Christmas decorations left in the attic or garage when you have finished. You should have all the contents for storage in boxes or containers, preferably with lids. They should all be in reasonable condition, so that they can be lifted easily and safely; they should all be clearly labelled with contents, showing whom the items are for, and suggesting what to do with them if they don't want them. It would also be very useful for you to keep a written list of the contents of the attic and garage, and to keep it readily available, both as a reminder for yourself and for you to remind your children and other relatives that they need to remove their possessions from your home. Of course you can have lists on your computer, and you could type them up if you wish, as typed lists can be neater and easier to read too. You could also do copies for your family.

CHAPTER SIX

Photos

Photos are an absolute nightmare! They need a whole chapter to themselves!

Sorting photos can be extremely interesting and distracting, but also very emotionally draining and time-consuming due to the vast range of memories they evoke. This can be especially difficult if there is a large quantity of them.

Ideally, all the photos can be set aside until you feel stronger and are able to deal with them. Just ensure that they are all kept safely together.

Photos with Just Scenery: These could be thrown away if they don't mean anything to you any more, or to anyone else.

Photos of Friends and Relations: Keep these together, preferably each of them annotated with name(s), relationship(s), place, occasion and date.

All the photos which you would like to keep can be put on to memory cards, computers and backup disks, so that you never lose them. Also, your family and friends can have copies which are easily accessible and do not take up any space!

If you would like to keep them as real photos, then you can if you wish, but it might be easier to have them categorised. For example, photos of friends kept together in one box; family photos in another.

I feel that it is really important to know where you come from, and therefore family photos of previous generations are vitally important. If possible, store them safely with any relevant details, such as names, as well as dates and places of birth, marriage and death.

CHAPTER SEVEN

Babies and Young Children

If you have babies and young children, it can be very hard to let go of any of their personal possessions, no matter what they are. It may also be completely impossible to find any spare time to sort through their belongings. You may like to keep everything, especially if you would like another baby.

When any clothing is outgrown, you can store it in a labelled container with a lid, or a box, stating what is inside. You can do the same with any outgrown toys, books and bedding too, putting all these items in the attic.

I would define a young child as a child who still attends primary school, up to the end of their time at primary school.

Although they may not yet be sixteen, the legal age of consent, I feel very strongly that they need to be involved with sorting out any of their possessions, and that it needs to be their decision to let their belongings go to somewhere else, NOT yours.

Their possessions belong to your child, and may hold fond memories for them, so if you get rid of their belongings without consulting them this may place a barrier between you.

It may be hard to bridge this barrier and repair the emotional damage that has been caused, as they may feel that they are no longer able to trust you. This trust is a fundamental foundation of your relationship with your growing child, which isn't easily regained, especially as they approach the more difficult and tempestuous teenage years.

Before this breach of trust occurred, your child felt secure and safe with you, and was able to discuss anything with you. Afterwards, they may not do so; they may even suffer from nightmares, pine for what they have lost and be afraid to leave their room for fear of returning to more missing possessions!

You need to prevent this from occurring by involving them in a sort-out if necessary. Even though they may have far too many belongings, and it annoys and frustrates you greatly, you need to be patient and await their co-operation in this process.

You may discover that this suddenly happens soon after they start to attend 'big school', as they may want to feel more grown-up. However, if the opposite is now true and they want to dispose of everything, discuss with them what may be worth keeping, especially as some well-cared-for toys may become collectors' pieces in the future. Also discuss which of their toys or books they might like to keep for their own potential future children.

All that you can do in the meantime is try to train them to place their toys in toy boxes, to tidy up and put toys away when they have finished using them, especially at the end of the day.

If you are young, working and have a young family, it can be very difficult, if not impossible, to find any spare time to sort through anything. Also, your free time is very precious and should be spent enjoying your children and family, giving them and you the quality time that you all deserve. This book is therefore probably aimed more at those in the fifty-plus age bracket, but may be useful to you in the future.

CHAPTER EIGHT

Our Own Experience of Decluttering

General Rules

Right from the beginning, if any of us found anything which could be of interest to the others, we placed the pieces in a clearly labelled crate or box, and put them in a mutually convenient and prominent place. For David, this was in his old bedroom, as this room was comparatively clear of junk and quite spacious. Whereas, for myself, this was usually the lounge, owing to the total chaos which prevailed in my old bedroom!

We ensured that we both knew where these items were put, by also entering the relevant information in the Communications Book, kept on the side in the kitchen. We always consulted this before we proceeded with the plan for each day.

Photos

As we both knew there would be an enormous number of photos, as both of our parents were enthusiastic photographers, we had to agree on who would deal with them at the start. I decided to undertake this task as I lived nearby, so I could take some home with me each time we visited Mum's house to clear it.

Indeed, although I visited Mum's house three times a week, almost every single visit for at least seven months yielded more photos! Every time we found some, whether they were photos in packets, by themselves, as slides or in albums, they were packed up together in crates and bags and I brought them home with me.

I often wondered what I had done by agreeing to this task, as this was a massive challenge: there were literally thousands of them! We stored them all in our conservatory until I had any spare time to sort through them. As I did not like seeing them all there, taking up so much space, nearly every evening, after our tea, I sorted through them. Our mum died in the August, and I was probably sorting photos from the middle of September until at least March the following year, daily, except for weekends and holidays, including Christmas, although I had Christmas Eve and Christmas Day off! Obviously, this meant that I didn't have much quality time with my own family, and I missed spending time with them dreadfully.

Any photos of possible interest to David I returned to the house and left in his old bedroom, for his perusal. Eventually David and I divided up several albums between us for each of us to keep, rather than splitting up the actual albums. That was what felt better for us to do.

All the photos were dealt with as described in Chapter Six.

Task by Task, Room by Room
I would like to explain, with a few examples of our own, how we sorted and cleared our mum's house, but I do not mean any disrespect to our late mum by doing so.

As mentioned earlier, although we had intended to do the sorting room by room, this was made impossible by the vast number of books found in the lounge, which covered almost every surface! There were over 1,000, so they filled a lot of the space. This example demonstrates that you have to be able to respond to whatever situation and circumstance you find yourself in; you have to be flexible and able to adapt to whatever arises.

The Downstairs

Books

We had to check every single book for any enclosed paperwork, and almost all of them had some paper inside, usually on the subject relevant to the book. The paperwork was read when found, and either kept back to read again or disposed of in the recycling.

The books were then checked for condition and put in appropriate piles for the library, playgroup, schools and charity shops. Any books which we were interested in, we kept back to take home with us to read.

Once these books were disposed of we did find more in various rooms and cupboards when we cleared each room; some of them we had never seen before, and some were even from our childhood!

Furniture

As David is really adept on the computer and has plenty of experience selling items via the Internet, much of the furniture was advertised for sale this way. Each piece of furniture had to be dealt with according to the order they were advertised for sale; because of this, Carole and I were kept extremely busy emptying it all!

It is very important for each of you to work to your best strengths, which is what we all did. Even though the fairly rapid sale of the furniture caused more chaos in the short term, with all the disgorged contents spread over the lounge floor, in the long term it was a huge relief as the furniture took up a lot of room and was usually fairly heavy. The newly 'homeless' contents were then sorted through, as previously described.

The Lounge

Once the books and some of the furniture had been removed, this instantly created more space in what was a really large lounge, although it had become an extremely cluttered room. This meant that we could now clearly see which tasks were ahead of us, instead of feeling as if we were being suffocated and trapped by all the mess.

Therefore our morale increased and we felt more motivated to continue with our arduous task. As a result, although there was still plenty to do, our speed of sorting and decision-making increased too. Henceforth, sorting through each piece of furniture almost became joyful as each item of furniture which had been dealt with became one more we had done and one less to do. By using this method of focusing on one job at a time, we could remain positive instead of dwelling on how much there was still to do and becoming anxious and stressed, as well as very negative and disheartened.

The Dining Room

Fortunately, all the furniture in the dining room was sold and removed quite quickly; and once the floor was cleaned properly, we had a wonderful space which was ideal for storage! As the dining room adjoined the lounge, this was perfect to act as a collection point for all the items which were packed up to go to various charities. Each time the dining room became two-thirds full, we arranged for another collection! Often by the collection date it was overflowing into the lounge!

The Study

The study was probably our worst room as it was very small and at first we could hardly open the door! It was blocked by loads of paperwork, so we initially grabbed handfuls of the paper and deposited it in the lounge until we could fully open the door. Once we had done that we progressed to using more convenient trayfuls! Fortunately for us the chairs and settee in the lounge were still in situ, so we could peruse the plentiful paperwork in relative comfort.

However, we had to read each and every piece of paper, so it took a very long time. Once read, we allocated them to the appropriate piles: different associations; important and to be kept safely; as well as junk mail and any recycling. The paperwork for the different associations was reread and forwarded to the appropriate groups, whilst the junk mail was recycled.

This small room took two of us about two weeks to clear! Although it was the smallest room, it was definitely the hardest. We found a bountiful supply of stationery items, all of which we split three ways for us to use; the good-quality remnants were donated to charity shops. We discovered a long-buried bookshelf, with accompanying books, which I had forgotten existed!

However, our most shocking concern was that all the plugs and sockets had been overwhelmed by paperwork: they had been made invisible by the depth of the paperwork for a very long-time. Once they had all been relieved of their huge burden, we felt all of them with our hands: all of them were extremely hot! I was so relieved that we had decided to do this room when we did, as it was obviously a fire waiting to happen!

We also rediscovered the almost buried filing cabinet, which contained much of the paperwork which was necessary to sell the house. This cabinet took a long time to deal with, but we were so relieved to have found everything: it was all kept together, and kept safely too. This certainly relieved some of my stress, as it was crucial to the sale of the house.

The Kitchen

The kitchen was an awful room to do, as every cupboard and drawer was full to capacity and beyond! Three of us did the kitchen, and it was sorted so much more quickly than we'd anticipated, with the extra pair of hands.

Old and out-of-date food tins and packets were disposed of in the rubbish; anything which could be used was divided amongst us and the neighbours. Any kitchenalia which we would like was kept back and allocated appropriately; everything else was either thrown in the rubbish, recycled or placed in the charity-shop pile.

The fridge was emptied and food distributed, if appropriate, amongst ourselves; the rest was discarded in the rubbish. Once the fridge was empty, the power was turned off and the plug disconnected, so it could be safely and thoroughly cleaned and disinfected. Afterwards we only used it for the bare essentials of a small amount of milk and bread, plus storing our packed lunches for the duration of the house clearance.

Once everywhere was empty in the kitchen, all the surfaces, cupboards and drawers were rigorously cleaned and disinfected, and the floor too. We only left what was essential equipment to use: mugs, the bare minimum of cutlery, bags for tea, coffee and sugar, and a few pieces of crockery. We also left the kitchen bin, kettle and radio. There was also extra space for a 'quick-find' stationery tray containing various pens, scissors, paper, notebooks and the essential Communications Book.

The Utility Room
A similar process of sorting to that which we used for the kitchen was adopted in the utility room too. However, as this was a small room, there was only just enough space in it for two of us at any one time. As this was often a squash, we adapted and used a relay system too.

We emptied the freezer, and I used all the fruit over a few months, with my family, baking delicious apple and blackcurrant crumbles! We also used all the vegetables. The freezer was treated in the same manner as the kitchen fridge. However, it was left unplugged, ready for later disposal by the council, as it was extremely old and rusty.

We also found a plentiful supply of cleaning products, as well as kitchen and baking wrappings, all of which were divided up between three of us once more.

The Understairs Cupboard
The understairs cupboard was a shock, as it was also completely full! This took quite a long time to empty and contained a wide range of eclectic belongings: a vast selection of different types of alcohol, all unopened; food tins and packages; very old books from our childhood; and a variety of lights.

We used the same method of sorting for these as we had used for all the other rooms. The alcohol was very interesting, but although the majority of spirits were in good condition and drinkable the same could not be said for almost all of the wine! When we attempted to taste some of the wine at home, it had gone off, so we had to tip it down the drain, which was such a shame. Our house did smell a bit like a brewery for a while!

The Upstairs

As we had now completed almost all of the clearing and cleaning for downstairs, except for leaving the essential pieces of equipment required by us for cleaning and nourishment, plus much of the lounge furniture, we could now proceed to work upstairs.

My Old Bedroom
My old bedroom was a large room, and we could only just get through the door! It looked as if the attic had been dumped into it, as all the floor, all surfaces and both beds were covered with an eclectic variety of items.

It took us a long time to work our way through it all, and we were forced by lack of space to start from the doorway, bags and boxes at the ready! We sorted through it in a methodical fashion, as previously described, especially as this was the only way we could hope to have some form of control over the chaos, and to retain our sanity!

In this room were two big wardrobes, four big cupboards, three sets of drawers and two beds, one of which had drawers under the bed too. We didn't bother investigating any of these until both the floor space and the beds were cleared of clutter. As our time was very precious, we had to make the best use of the time that we did have there, which meant not getting unduly distracted by adding to the mess which was already in front of us. Once again, the room was given a fairly good clean before we began emptying the furniture. After the contents of the furniture were dealt with, and the room was cleaned again, we felt ready to confront the attic contents.

The Attic
As my old bedroom was now mainly empty, except for the furniture, David brought the entire contents of the attic into it, which made it almost full again! However, this wasn't nearly as bad as we had anticipated, as all of it was boxed in lidded containers.

As a result, this was much easier and quicker to sort through, and both David and I had some lidded containers each, eventually.

The Airing Cupboard
Inside the airing cupboard we found loads of bedding, towels and toiletries. Most of the bedding and towels were sent to the charity shop, or used for either our or the neighbours' dog. However, some were old-style and embroidered, so these were sold to collectors via an old school friend of mine.

To our dismay though, there were three huge crates of toiletries: all were unopened and unused! We divided all of these between the three of us once more unless they had passed their use-by dates, in which case they were disposed of in the rubbish.

The Bathroom
The bathroom was relatively easy to clear, as it was a small room. However, the under-sink cupboard revealed more hidden medicines!

It was only necessary to retain a few towels, toilet rolls

and cleaning and washing essentials in here until the house was completely emptied.

Mum's Old Bedroom

Mum's old bedroom was left until last, as we all found it very hard to do, with all the memories it contained. Also, as the bed was still in situ, it felt very much as if Mum was still there or about to return; this obviously felt rather unnerving and strange.

It was very quiet in here, and as I started doing this room by myself, alone in the house, I felt very melancholic and thoughtful, plus I felt a deep sense of loss. I felt as if Mum's essence was retained in this room, and that by clearing it I was invading her privacy, as well as losing her all over again.

As I disliked the complete silence which surrounded me, I plugged in a radio to keep me company. This also alleviated some of my sadness. The station played jolly and uplifting music, which also helped to motivate me.

In this room there were four above-the-bed cupboards, two large and deep wardrobes, two smaller wardrobes, two sets of bedside drawers as well as numerous other drawers and four under-the-bed drawers.

First of all the bedroom shelves and surfaces were cleared of ornaments and bric-a-brac, which was carefully wrapped, labelled and stored safely in order to avoid breakages caused by our decluttering. Only when this was completed could we do any further sorting.

The above-the-bed cupboards were emptied first and all the contents laid out on the bed for sorting through. Any items which I was unsure of were boxed up ready for inspection by the others, and put to one side. The smaller wardrobes were next: one had a dilapidated set of drawers inside, which contained a huge amount of paper stationery, much of which was usable. This was again split up between the three of us who would use it. Anything found which was unsuitable for use was recycled or thrown in the rubbish. The set of drawers was removed from the room and placed in the garage to await collection by the council. Enclosed in the other wardrobes was a large quantity of clothes and footwear. Most of these were sent to the charity shop, except for those we wanted to keep. After the wardrobes, we tackled numerous sets of drawers all around the room, which took quite a long time due to the large number and variety of items found within.

Any jewellery we found was kept together in lidded crates for me to take home and keep safely until David and I had enough time together to sort through it.

When we had cleared all of this, we pulled out the bed and discovered that all four under-the-bed drawers were full to bursting point – so much so that they were almost impossible to open. How they had ever been closed in the first place was beyond our comprehension! As before, we utilised the extra space and easy working height which the bed gave us in order to sort the contents. Many of these items were brand new and still in their original packaging! The next task was the bedside drawers, which, once again, contained an astonishing amount for such a small space.

After the bedside drawers were moved away from the positions they had maintained for very many years, we discovered some previously almost hidden storage cupboards! Our dad had been an enthusiastic do-it-yourself man, and had built almost all of the bedroom furniture, which encompassed many original features! We found yet more medicines here too. It would have been impossible to reach for our mum, so it was extremely puzzling about when and how the medicines were put in here.

After cleaning this room thoroughly, we felt deeply satisfied with what we had achieved, but I also felt rather sad as it no longer felt like Mum's room now that it was empty and depersonalised.

David

As David had a full-time job and I didn't, he had to attend to his work as well as helping us with decluttering and sorting Mum's house. This is the reason why we sorted through the majority of the inside of the house by ourselves.

However, he assisted us enormously by selling much of the furniture, sorting his old bedroom, emptying the attic contents so that we could clear it and finding a home for much of the remaining furniture by using it himself; he also took on the garage and both the sheds, plus the garden paraphernalia, mostly by himself. The garage and sheds were horrendous to clear, as they were all packed to the brim and beyond.

The Garage

The garage was absolutely dreadful, as it was packed to the rafters and beyond: we couldn't see out of the window! It was very dark and gloomy – a depressing and 'suffocating' place to be in, as well as being a site of a potential accident waiting to happen due to all the debris and junk you had to very carefully step over if you needed anything! However, it was also very like an

Aladdin's cave as David never knew what he was going to find.

I was so grateful that David decided to do this, as I am not sure that I would have had the patience.

There were many items which had to be taken to the tip; the rest was recycled or thrown in the rubbish. We also held two or three garage sales, which were very successful. However, we had to hire a skip to dispose of some of the larger items and most of the rubbish which couldn't easily be recycled.

The Sheds and Garden Paraphernalia

David also found a very useful free-to-collect site for many of the pots and other containers in the garden, which he advertised and people came to collect them. It was also through this site that we found a new home for some of Dad's photography equipment, with a young photography student; we think that Dad would have been pleased that it has been put to good use.

House-Clearance Companies

Although the convenience, including time- and labour-saving benefits, of having one of these firms did appeal to us, neither of us even considered having them, in spite of the numerous offers made. This was because we both felt that hiring one of them would amount to an invasion of our privacy in our much loved former family home. Being there, surrounded by our parents' possessions, meant that we were able to start to grieve for our mum, as well as our life as a family, including our dad too.

We could be left in peace to try to come to terms with it all by sorting through their belongings, remembering happier times as we did so.

Our mum would certainly not have approved of having strangers in her home either. We would also have lost far too much which was precious to us – so many lost memories and possessions, some of which we had never seen before.

It would be entirely up to each of you whether to hire a house-clearance firm, but, before you do, remember just how many of those happy memories you could lose by doing so. Would you regret that decision in the future?

CHAPTER NINE

How to Keep Your Home Clutter-Free

General Tips

In order to keep your home tidy after all your hard work, you now need to begin a new routine. Once you have finished using or looking at something, you need to put it away where it belongs. This applies for all occasions and situations, such as after shopping trips, days out and holidays too.

If you and everyone you live with can do this, instead of continuing to pursue a 'drop and go' system, it will be much easier for all of you to find anything you need quickly, as well as to keep your home clean.

1. DO NOT be tempted to refill the space you have made.

2. Sort through post on the day that it arrives. Depending on what it is, recycle it, rip it up and put in the kitchen waste bin, shred it or deal with it as appropriate. Never let it start to pile up and always write the date received on the envelope so it is dealt with in order.

3. Old tea towels and hand towels can be used as floorcloths or other cleaning cloths, perhaps in the utility room, for lining and protecting kitchen drawers and cupboards, or any other spaces which could be susceptible to the damp, or used as dog towels.

4. Old bath towels and old bedding, especially if worn out and stained, can be used as floor or furniture protectors when decorating, or as dog towels and bedding.

5. After you have thoroughly cleaned each room, review the contents of the room and recycle or reallocate unused items, as described earlier.

6. Every six months, sort through your books, DVDs and CDs. Once a year, sort through your clothes, jewellery, bric-a-brac, kitchen, garage and attic, and recycle or reallocate unused items.

Future-Proofing

Organ Donation

If you are able to, discuss your views on possible organ donation with family and friends, so they are aware of your wishes in the event of your death. You can explain your reasons to them for wanting to become a donor, which may alleviate some of their own concerns and anxieties regarding this strongly emotive issue.

Ensure that you are registered as a donor and always carry your donor card with you.

Prepayment Funeral Plans

You can collect information regarding prepayment funeral plans from several different funeral directors. Once you know what you want, you can either pay into the plan by instalments or pay in full. This is much easier to do whilst you are fit and well, rather than extremely ill, in pain and possibly close to death. This will help you to have peace of mind and will ultimately save you and your relatives money in the long term. The cost of funerals is always increasing, so you will pay at the current rate, not the rate which will be charged in the future.

By doing this now, it means that you can discuss your wishes with your family and friends and inform them that your funeral has already been paid for and arranged. You can even choose your own hymns! As funerals are obviously very sad events, this will relieve some of the financial and emotional hardship, stress and strain for all those who care for you. This will also stop or prevent any arguments about your wishes, as you have already stated what you want. Inform your family and friends about the funeral details and where they can be found.

Make a Will

Ensure that you have made a will and that it is up to date. It is really important, as if you die without a will your next of kin will not get what you would like them to, and the taxman will benefit instead! Ensure that you have discussed this with your family, and that they know who your solicitor is and their contact details, as well as where to find a copy of your latest will.

An Up-To-Date Address Book

Ensure that you have one main address book and that it is up to date, for ease of contacting relatives, friends and businesses, such as banks and solicitors. It may also be useful to put what the relationship to you is, in brackets, next to each address. You can always have a shorter version kept near the telephone table.

I found that doing this was like a spring clean in itself, as my previous address book dated from when I was in my twenties! It is so much easier to find the information I need now that I can't believe it took me so many years to do it. However, as I was sentimentally attached to my old book, it was very hard for me to let it go.

An Up-To-Date Contacts List

It is important to have an up-to-date contacts list for bank accounts and any other financial business, so that it is easier for your executors to deal with. Keep this list in a safe place. Also, ensure that your bank and business accounts are up to date at all times. Perhaps try and update them once a month, and ensure that you shred any unwanted paperwork afterwards to avoid the possibility of your identity being stolen.

Important Documents

Always ensure that your family know where all your important documents are kept. This is so important: it is essential that you do this, as mentioned earlier.

A House File

Have a file about your house. This is important too, as your family and potential buyers will need to know various important pieces of information.

1. Information about any building works that you have had done including names and contact details of all firms used, with dates and works completed. Include

extra information regarding the quality of the work and if you would recommend the contractor in the future, as well as any warranties, guarantees or certificates for the work. Another good idea is to state where the load-bearing or supporting walls are in your property too.

2. Contact details for all your utility companies, as well as emergency contact numbers for each one.

3. The locations of cables and pipework for the gas, electric, water and phone, both inside and outside the property, including stopcocks and water meter, if there is one.

4. Details of your heating system, including installation, servicing and operating manuals for your boiler. Give details of who services the heating system and when it is next due for a service.

5. Details of the installation and service history of your burglar alarm, including its operating manual. The code would be useful to any new buyers, but do not record it here at present; in the meantime, just ensure that your immediate family and any other keyholders have the code.

6. Details of the banding rate of the property, and a short history of increases in the community charge through previous years (this can be just a short written list).

7. Provide all manuals, guarantees and service histories for appliances staying in the property.

8. Contact details for county and town councils.

9. Contact details for GP surgeries, schools, libraries, dustbin and recycling collection days and times. Information about what shops and other facilities are available near the property. Perhaps include any local free newspapers and magazines too, plus a map of the town if there is one.

Family Medical History

It might be useful to have a record of your family medical history, for your relatives, for their information in the future. The details should include full names, as well as dates of birth and death.

You should mention any medical conditions suffered for each person, including any family hereditary conditions (such as heart conditions and pre-eclampsia), plus eczema, hayfever and asthma. You also need to state any important allergies, such as nuts, penicillin or bee stings.

Your Children's Health Records

Instead of just recording all of their important milestones in the Health Visitor book, issued when they were born, you could improve upon this by using a small hardback notebook for each of your children. This could include their blood type, if known, and any allergies, illnesses and vaccinations, making note of treatments and reactions. You could also record extra milestones, such as their first day at school or the first time they read a word or rode a bike.

This may be interesting for them to read when they have their own children, and can be useful for them to use as a reference tool if they become concerned about them.

An Information Sheet for Possessions to be Kept

An information sheet may be useful for your next of kin in order for them to be able to decide what to do with your possessions. Once again, this could help to reduce some of their stress, too.

If possible, provide:

- Name of manufacturer and date.
- What the piece is made from.
- When and where it was bought
- The original purchase price, plus receipt and guarantee, if available.
- A list of instructions about what to do with each piece if it is unwanted by family members or friends. (Remember, the tastes of your family and friends may be totally different from your own.) An idea for a list of possible outlets is given in Chapter Four.

YOUR BIOGRAPHY

Preferably, you should be able to discuss your life story with your family, but, as a 'keepsake' addition to these conversations, you can leave them a written record of your own life. This may be something which gives them comfort in the future, after your own demise, and it could also be used as a eulogy at your own funeral!

You could begin by writing a short record of your life, perhaps with a timeline included, with years and ages, beginning with your birth and early upbringing and showing any house and school moves, and recording brief details of your life as an adult too.

You can then expand on this, by giving more details of your life at each stage, such as what you played with as a child; any special, funny or embarrassing memories; your later education, plus any interests and hobbies; what jobs you have done as an adult; how you met your partner or why you decided to stay single; your interests and hobbies as you grew older; any animals you have owned; where you have visited and taken holidays; and any other notable life events and how they affected you. Include any memorable journeys and experiences which helped to shape you into the person that you have become.

As you can see, the list is pretty much endless, as there are so many different possibilities. Remember, it is entirely up to you what you write, but your family will be really thankful.

CONCLUSION

As I have always been a little bit of a hoarder, it used to be very difficult to throw anything away and I dreaded the annual sort-out of our attic. However, since helping to declutter my late mum's home, which was packed to the brim with everything, I have been able to re-evaluate what is important to keep in our own home.

Having gone through our own home thoroughly, twice, from bottom to top and vice versa, including the attic, every room is now under constant review, and I nearly always have a bag on the go for the charity shop!

Now that I have learnt from my experiences at Mum's house and, as a result, have become a declutterer, it has transformed my life. I now feel so much better. I love life once more. Our house is much cleaner and I am so much happier; I feel so positive about everything and everyone. At long last, I now have time for myself, and I have joined two local groups, which I thoroughly enjoy.

Become a declutterer and change your life for the better too!

EPILOGUE

I hope that this book has helped you all to find which belongings you really care about and would like to keep, to look after them properly, as well as motivating you to dispose of items which you don't need.

Do you all feel better in yourselves now, compared to when you began your sorting?

I couldn't believe how much better I felt afterwards: I literally felt like a different person; I felt as if I could breathe freely again! I felt so much lighter as the weight created by stress in my head, neck and shoulders had vanished!

After Mum's house, we decluttered our own home too, which was amazing as I had a completely new attitude and approach to it. Instead of dreading it, I couldn't wait to face the challenge!

Becoming an enthusiastic declutterer has transformed my life. I am much happier and feel more like the real me – something I haven't felt for a very long time. Surprisingly, getting rid of our clutter has had another unexpected benefit for me: it has released me from a long-term depression, which I hadn't realised I suffered from, following a close-together double family loss twenty years ago! I had always felt that something was holding

72

me back, but didn't know what it was until it had gone.

I do need to admit though, that even now our house is not always tidy as we all lead very busy lives, but it is much better than it used to be. I do get told off for putting things away too quickly! I also have one messy drawer and one messy cupboard, both of which are sorted and tidied every so often, when the chaos inside becomes too much to bear! These are not really intentional – it is just that they become like this very rapidly after sorting. This is due to very frequent use by everyone, and an abundance of Tupperware containers, all of which are used at various times by different family members, making it impossible to discard any!

FURTHER READING

The Life-Changing Magic of Tidying by Marie Kondo.
The Tidy Closet by Marie-Anne Lecoeur.

ACKNOWLEDGEMENTS

I would like to say a huge thank you to all the people who read the first draft of this book and gave constructive and creative advice and feedback, all of which I have tried to act upon and include in this final draft.

Most of these people are already mentioned in the dedication, but they also include Will Greene; Hayley Pollard and all the staff at the St Luke's Charity Shop, Saltash; Debbie and Andrew at The Bookshelf, Saltash; Diane Shann and Mary Grant of Trematon WI, Saltash, plus their friends Ronnie and Tim; and last, but not least, Julie Rance, of Livewire Youth Project, Saltash, who encouraged me to continue writing, and also wanted to go home and declutter straight away!

An enormous **thank you** to our near neighbours and friends, Gill and Jill, for their invaluable insight and for discovering a very important, but absent, element to include in my final draft. Hence, the extended Chapter Three and Chapter Eight, 'Our Own Experience of Decluttering', are dedicated to them.

I would also like to say a great big **thank you** to the staff at Speedy Prints, Saltash, for all their help and patience for printing numerous draft copies and reprints for this book.

And, finally, I need to say a **GIGANTIC THANK YOU** to my son, Matthew, for his endless hours of patience and kindness, for helping to teach me how to use the computer properly, even though I tested his patience to the extreme at times; and he did this even though he was also studying for his AS levels and now his A levels! What a hero! I really couldn't have done this without you.